DEFINE YOU

A 40-Day Biblical Challenge to Claim and Manifest Your God-Given Destiny!

Chris Noble

DEFINE YOU

A 40-Day Biblical Challenge to Claim and Manifest Your God-Given Destiny!

Scripture Quotations

Published by

Chris Noble Christian Life Coaching

www.ChrisNobleCLC.com

ISBN: 979-8-89525-438-7

Printed in the United States of America

Dedication

I want to express my sincere gratitude, first and foremost, to God, without whom I can do nothing, to my loving parents, Clyde and Mary Noble, my brother Clyde Noble, Jr., and to all who have had a positive impact on my life by instilling Christian values, wisdom, and encouragement. You have been my steadfast companions through thick and thin, and I thank God for you.

Dad has gone home to be with the Lord, and although I regret that I can no longer talk with him, I treasure the integrity, strong work ethic, positive attitude, faith, lessons, hopes, and dreams he and my mother fostered in me. I pray that the life I live and the service I give will always honor God and my parents.

With Love Forever,
Chris Noble, Your Fearless Son

Acknowledgment

The Bible contains many verses that promise that if you follow God's guidance, everything will fall into place to help you live out your God-given purpose. That statement is personified in the person of my pastor, spiritual leader, teacher, and friend, Dr. Veronica Thomas Jackson. She has taught me so much! Her grace and love for God and His people are unwavering. I speak abundant blessings, healing, and peace over her as she continues to be a "Christian Renaissance Woman!"

Love and Thanks,
Chris Noble

About the Author

Chris Noble stands as a beacon of hope in business leadership, defying the limits of one's humble circumstances to carve out a promising future. As a Young Adult Ministry leader, he is passionate about guiding young adults past their hurdles and is dedicated to their personal and professional growth.

With over two decades of entrepreneurial triumphs, Noble brings expertise to empower those striving for more. His credentials include diplomas in Practical Theology and Personal Development and Christian Ministry and Leadership from the North Carolina School of Ministry and Leadership.

Beyond his business acumen, Noble serves as a seasoned Christian leader and messenger of God's teachings. As a motivational speaker, he fervently encourages individuals to unlock their fullest potential through faith and determination.

www.ChrisNobleCLC.com

Table of Contents

Introduction

It has been said that "It takes one to know one," which can be interpreted in various ways. Typically, it means that a person's character, energy, or vibe can identify a similar trait in someone else. To do this, you must confidently and unapologetically know who you are. It's about embracing that you are a unique, one-of-a-kind person created for a specific purpose. Unfortunately, many people don't understand how to discover their purpose. They tend to follow the latest trends or what works for others without considering whether it is God's will for their life.

Over the next 40 days, you will embark on a spiritual journey to define yourself and live your best life. The 40-day challenge is significant because it symbolizes a period of testing, trial, and triumph in the Bible. Jesus wandered in the wilderness for 40 days, God flooded the earth for 40 days and nights, and Moses fasted for 40 days. Spiritually speaking, the number "40" suggests transformation.

Don't let the word "challenge" intimidate you. Challenges are opportunities for growth. They're necessary for us to become our best selves. But to realize our purpose, dreams, goals, and aspirations, we must believe we can do so by focusing our thoughts and energy in that direction. The Bible warns that faith without works is dead, and idleness has many unfavorable consequences. A victorious Christian life is characterized by prayer, faith, obedience, diligence, stewardship, and responsibility.

Remember:

We can do all things through Christ, who strengthens us.
Philippians 4:13

First Things First

If you do not know Jesus as your Lord and Savior, I encourage you to pray this prayer in faith and start your new life in Christ. God will save and help you right now where you are.

A Prayer for Salvation

Dear God, I come to you in the name of Jesus. I admit that I am not right with you, but today, I repent and ask you to forgive me. I believe Jesus died for my sins and rose from the dead. I invite You to come into my heart and life, save me, and fill me with Your Holy Spirit. Today, I trust, receive, and confess You as my Lord and Savior. Thank you, God, for saving me. In Jesus' name. Amen.

If you prayed that simple prayer in faith, you have been born again. God has tossed all your sins into the sea of forgetfulness and will remember them no more. You have entered a personal relationship with Jesus Christ. Give God first place in your life. Learn to pray and join a Bible-believing church where you can be baptized and continue to grow in grace.

As a believer in Christ, you are granted the gift of the Holy Spirit, who will be with you on your 40-day journey to give you strength, courage, and guidance to claim and manifest the life you were born to live. Call on Jesus. He is there now and for eternity with a promise never to leave or forsake you.

Getting Started on Your Spiritual Journey

But seek ye first the kingdom of God, and his righteousness; and all these things shall be added unto you. -**Matthew 6:33**

Discerning God's will (what He wants) and purpose (what He plans) for your life isn't always easy, but it's ultimately worth it. As you walk by faith, you will mature spiritually, grow stronger and closer to Him, and learn to follow where He leads.

Let's look at two types of God's will. God's sovereign will is God's divine and perfect plan for your life. The permissive will of God is what He permits us to do outside His perfect will. There can be adverse consequences when we go outside the perfect will of God. Obedience to God's sovereign will for our lives is necessary to enjoy the benefits of His divine will and plan for us.

In essence, the Word of God is His sovereign will. While there aren't precise instructions in the Bible for every scenario that may arise in your life, you can see God's will by studying His Word and knowing His character. You will learn what pleases God as you get to know Him better. Here are some additional pointers:

- Make sure your decisions line up with the Word of God.
- Ensure the scripture you base your decision on applies to your situation.
- It's important to listen to your thoughts and emotions, but PRAY about them so you won't mistake these things for the voice of God.
- We should always consider how our decisions affect others, but you cannot always please people. Your goal, therefore, should be to please God.
- God desires us to know and do His will. He's not trying to hide anything from you. The Bible tells us not to worry about anything, to pray about everything, and to expect God to answer.
- Talk and pray with other mature Christian friends for confirmation, but don't let others

decide for you. You are responsible for the decisions you make.

- God can open doors; no one can close and close doors; no one can open, but every obstacle isn't a closed door. Don't let circumstances make your decisions. God can make a way out of no way. Learn to wait on the Lord.
- Remember, when you gave your life to God, He came into your head and heart. Use your sanctified common sense as you prayerfully move forward.
- Once you discern God's will, know He will enable you to do whatever He calls you to do. He is always in control.

YOUR CHALLENGE

How to Discern God's Purpose for Your Life

This 40-day challenge aims to help you discover, claim, and begin living out God's divine will and purpose for your life. A clear sense of purpose is essential for a happy, productive life. Again, remember to immerse yourself in God's Word and prayer. Prayer will not only help you realize God's purpose for your life, it will help you live it. Now, it's time to consider the following:

Are you truly open to going where God leads you?

____

____

____

Have you ever felt that God was leading you in a particular direction, but you didn't understand it until later? If so, what did you learn from that experience?

____

____

____

What are your gifts, talents, and interests?

What decisions or choices are you facing now?

What are your needs?

What are your values and beliefs?

What gives you a sense of purpose?

___

___

___

What do you enjoy?

___

___

___

What would you do if there were no limits?

___

___

___

How do you envision your life?

___

___

___

What DON'T you want?

Day 1

God's Word for You

Before I formed thee in the belly, I knew thee, and before thou camest forth out of the womb, I sanctified thee, and I ordained thee a prophet unto the nations.

-Jeremiah 1:5

Prayer

Father, I thank You for all You do. Thank You for always standing by my side, never leaving or forsaking me. I confess that I've sinned and fallen short of Your glory. Please forgive me. Open my mind as I face the challenges ahead. Grant me wisdom and strength to persevere and draw me closer to You. May I never give up, as You have never given up on me. You are an awesome, faithful, and promise-keeping God. I praise and thank You in advance for the victory and blessings on the way. In Jesus' name, I pray, Amen.

It's Your Time

Life is what you make it. You can choose to be a victim or a victor. If you're not where you want to be in life, you can blame others or change it. We can't fully control life, but we can control our response. Many people never pursue their dreams and goals. Some reasons include listening to failed attempt horror stories from others or never being told your past or present doesn't define your future. Be encouraged by the adage, "If at first, you don't succeed, try, try again."

Everyone wants the same things in life, just in different ways. What goals are you still hoping to obtain?

To find your purpose _________

To reach your full potential__________

Happiness__________

Health__________

Wealth__________

Success____________

Security____________

Meaningful Relationships__________

Peace of Mind_______________

Fear Chaser

Fear is a natural emotion with benefits and hidden facets. It creates caution when there is danger, but this emotion can also be activated when faced with something new or unknown. Past unpleasant experiences, such as trauma, often trigger fear.

While avoiding situations you fear may make you feel better in the short term, it can also block you from living the life you were born to live. To manifest the life you were born to live, you must address your goals and obstacles with honesty, vulnerability, and courage.

Contrary to popular belief, the thought of success can be scary for some, which leads to procrastination. Many also fear success because it can come with significant responsibilities that hold you to higher standards. Fear can make it easier to deflect responsibility and avoid potential consequences when things go wrong.

Start chasing your fears with positive thinking. All things are possible with God. Tell yourself you can do it and learn from your past regarding what not to do. Start doing the things you are afraid of and reach for your goals without a second thought. Remember these words when fear crosses your mind:

"I sought the Lord; He heard me and delivered me from all my fears." ***-Psalm 34:4***

"Fear thou not; for I am with thee: be not dismayed; for I am thy God: I will strengthen thee; yea, I will help thee; yea, I will uphold thee with the right hand of my righteousness." **- Isaiah 41:10**

YOUR CHALLENGE

Write at least five tasks you've been avoiding because of **FEAR.**

1)____

2)____

3)____

4)____

5)____

More?______________________________________

Today's Affirmation

God is my refuge and strength, a very present help.
(Psalm 46:1)

Day 2

God's Word for You

Remember ye, not the former things, neither consider the things of old. Behold, I will do a new thing; now it shall spring forth; shall ye not know it? I will even make a way in the wilderness and rivers in the desert.

-Isaiah 43: 18-19

Prayer

Father God, how excellent is Thy name in all the earth! I come to You today as a humble servant seeking forgiveness for my sins. Please strengthen me when I'm weak. Thank You for loving me unconditionally. I pray for wisdom and guidance in every area of my life. There are things I don't know or understand, but I know who will hold tomorrow. Thank you, God! Continue shaping me into your image and keep your arms of protection around me. Grant me faith and patience to wait on You. Remove anything that's not like You. Heal my mind and body. Help me to know and do Your will for Your glory. This is my prayer in Jesus' name. Amen.

Lessons or Weapons

Life can be an emotional roller coaster. Unfortunately, we don't have a rewind button to do things over. Constantly remembering your mistakes, failures, and bad choices results in living life in repeat mode, which prevents happiness and progression. Mistakes are part of the bigger picture no matter who or where you are in life. Learning from your mistakes prepares you for more extraordinary achievements. Every life experience shapes your character, has lessons to learn, and gives you a testimony to share with others. The past does not define who you are unless you allow it.

People may try to degrade you based on your past mistakes. Please don't listen to them. Your future is in God's hands, not theirs. No one is perfect. We all make mistakes. Learn from your mistakes, and remember, trials come to make you strong. Your past is a lesson for growth, not a weapon to keep you down.

The number one reason we have a hard time achieving our goals is because we're living in the past. Every day is a new beginning. Remember, the power of life and death is in the tongue. What we think is what we produce. Speak life into your situation. Let go of whatever is holding you back. Looking back is allowing your past to be used as a weapon to pull you back and keep you there. Whose report will you believe? God or the enemy?

Those in Christ should rejoice because the Bible says all things work together for good to those who love God. Not just good things, not some things, but ALL things work together for good to those who love God and are called according to His purposes. Every goal on your list is an individual piece of the puzzle that connects to one giant puzzle called life. Each obstacle we face is a required piece of the bigger picture. You can either learn from it and continue putting the puzzle together or allow each piece that was an obstacle to keep you stuck in that same spot. Practice letting whatever isn't a positive in your life GO! Notice how you feel as you forgive and empty the trash. You will soon recognize that every event has been carefully orchestrated to help you realize your limitless potential. The past should be celebrated in many ways as we see what the Lord has brought us through and where He has brought us from. The past teaches us how we've grown, what we've learned, and who we've become, all of which can help increase our confidence.

YOUR CHALLENGE

Write at least five lessons you've learned from the past.

1)____

____

____

2)____

____

____

3)____

____

____

4)____

____

____

5)____

____

____

More?____

____

____

Today's Affirmation

God has equipped me for every good work.
(Hebrews 13:21)

Day 3

God's Word for You

Be strong and of a good courage, fear not, nor be afraid of them: for the LORD thy God, He it is that doth go with thee; He will not fail thee, nor forsake thee.

-Deuteronomy 31:6

Prayer

Our Father, and our God, giver of every good and perfect gift. God of the heavens and earth. Thank you, Lord, for making ways out of no way.

Thank You for all Your many blessings. Thank you for the battles you're fighting on my behalf and the victories you've already won. Thank You for protecting me from seen and unseen dangers.

Forgive me, Father, for my sins of commission and omission. I pray for peace in knowing You have everything under control. Grant me faith, strength, and courage to stay out of Your way and to know which way to go.

Father, I ask You to heal the sick, discouraged, depressed, suffering, and those who don't know You. May all who are lost come to You seeking salvation. Thank You, Father, for all You have done, all You're going to do, and for all You're doing right now. In Jesus' name, Amen.

I Am Enough

Psalm 139:14 says: "I will praise thee; for I am fearfully and wonderfully made: marvelous are thy works; and that my soul knoweth right well. Amen."

God makes no mistakes. You are unique and one of a kind. You are God's masterpiece.

Are you guilty of comparing yourself to others?

The reality is most individuals wish they were like someone else. It's essential to define yourself as all you were created to be. Remember, God created you for a divine purpose, and everything you need is within you. Seek to know and stay in God's will to claim the life you were born to live. You will attract every resource needed, and with God's guidance, you can do what others say couldn't be done.

Remove the phrase "I WISH" from your vocabulary. Trade the mindset of "I WISH" for an "I CAN" and an "I AM" mindset.

I Am Bold and Courageous!

I Have Faith in God and Myself!

I Am Blessed and Highly Favored!

YOUR CHALLENGE

Write at least three areas that you are SELF-CONSCIOUS about and want to improve to claim and manifest the life you were born to live.

1)____

____

____

2)____

____

____

3)____

____

____

Today's Affirmation

I can do all things through Christ
who strengthens me.
(Philippians 4:13)

Day 4

God's Word for You

Give instruction to a wise man, and he will be yet wiser: teach a just man, and he will increase in learning.

-Proverbs 9:9

Prayer

Heavenly Father, thank You for Your unfailing love. Thank You for Your Word that reminds us of Your promises. All of our help comes from You. Thank You for walking with us. When we're right and even when we're wrong, you're always by our side. God, I ask for Your discernment and guidance through the Holy Spirit today. Open my eyes and help me to know Your will and Your way. Help me make wise decisions so I may be drawn closer to You. Your ways are perfect, Father. Help me lean not to my own understanding but to acknowledge You as You direct my path. In Jesus' name, I pray. Amen.

Are You the Company You Keep?

It has been said, "If you're the smartest person in the room, you're in the wrong room." Surrounding ourselves with people who are more intelligent or think differently challenges us to "level up." This quote isn't new, but it's relevant. Being with the same people or people with similar values doesn't promote growth. We risk becoming a clone of everyone else without realizing it. Humans constantly mirror each other. Being the most intelligent person in the room is our comfort zone because we don't have to perform at our best. The beginning of growth is when we become fearless and welcome new encounters. Seeking higher minds leads to higher grounds. Put your anxiety in your pocket, stop hiding, say hello to someone new, and evolve!

YOUR CHALLENGE

Are there people in your life that you need to withdraw yourself from? YES or NO

If the answer is yes, why have you allowed them to be a part of your circle, and what are your plans to eliminate negativity to claim the life you were born to live?

____

____

____

Today's Affirmation

All of my help comes from the Lord.
(Psalm 121:2)

Day 5

God's Word for You

And Jesus said unto them, Because of your unbelief: for verily I say unto you, if ye have faith as a grain of mustard seed, ye shall say unto this mountain, Remove hence to yonder place; and it shall remove, and nothing shall be impossible unto you. **-Matthew 17:20**

Prayer

Dear Heavenly Father, creator and sustainer of all life, giver of every good and perfect gift: I acknowledge that Your will and plans for my life are greater than anything I could ever imagine, hope, or ask for. Today, I ask You to help everyone who is weighted down with care and trouble to put their trust in You. Please help them know that You are a burden bearer and a heavy load sharer. Help them see that You are a doctor who's never lost a case. May we learn to trust in You more and more each day. Help us, Father, to decrease that You may increase. Help us to be more like You. Help us believe that we are more than conquerors because of You! This is my prayer in Jesus' name. Amen.

Coming Soon

Failure is not a sign of weakness or inability to achieve your goals. Those who've accomplished incredible feats have done so because they refused to give up. We learn from our mistakes. You're not a failure as long as you keep trying. Unsuccessful attempts should be considered water under the bridge or a lesson learned. Don't allow something old to keep you in mental bondage, which can lead to giving up. Tomorrow is another day. If you can imagine yourself reaching a goal, you can do just that. Mistakes should be regarded as teaching opportunities rather than roadblocks. Everyone has, will, and continues to make mistakes consciously and unconsciously. No one on this earth is perfect. Don't let your mistakes define you or what people say discourage you. You must believe in God and yourself. Have confidence, pray, and practice positive thinking by faith. There is nothing too hard for our God. If He leads you to it, He'll bring you through it!

YOUR CHALLENGE

How do you interpret the phrase **"appeared to fail?"**

___

___

___

Write about a time when it "seemed" that you had failed but later learned that it prepared you for something greater.

___

___

___

___

___

Today's Affirmation

I am an overcomer.
(James 1:2-4)

Day 6

God's Word for You

Thou wilt keep him in perfect peace, whose mind is stayed on thee: because he trusteth in thee. Trust ye in the LORD forever: for in the LORD JEHOVAH is everlasting strength. ***-Isaiah 26:3-4***

Prayer

Dear God, I come to You acknowledging that Your will and plans are greater than anything I could ever ask, hope for, or imagine. Open my heart to sincerely receive Your Word that I might be a doer and not a hearer only. Increase my faith, Father, so that I might bear much fruit. Please show me the way to go and grant me peace. Give me eyes to see, ears to hear, and a heart to receive Your correction and guidance for Your glory. Father, this is my prayer in Jesus' name. Amen.

Focus

How many times have you looked at your social media today? Social media was designed to entertain, communicate with friends, and build new relationships. A study revealed that people spend an average of 2 hours and 26 minutes daily on social media. That's a lot of time if it's not productive. This virtual world can distract people to the point that they forget who they are. They forget about real issues and become entangled in competing with the online society and avoiding reality.

It promotes avoiding dealing with things humans don't like about themselves. Instead, people go online and present themselves how they want to be seen without making fundamental changes. This is dangerous and very deceptive. Individuals online appear flawless, but no one is perfect; even those who lead enviable lives have their struggles. Social media is a powerful tool, but it shouldn't be used to measure your success or define how your life should be.

Time is precious, and there are no "do-overs" in life. I challenge you to audit how your time is spent each day. Determine the amount of free time you have and what you are doing with it. Are you resting, gossiping, or creating a better you without the distractions of comparing yourself to others?

Focus, stay positive, and have faith so you can claim and achieve the life you were born to live.

YOUR CHALLENGE

List at least three distractions keeping you from achieving the life you were born to live.

1)____

____

____

2)____

____

____

3)____

____

____

More?___________________________________

____

____

Today's Affirmation

I serve an on-time God.
(Habakkuk 2:3)

Day 7

God's Word for You

And we know that all things work together for good to them that love God, to them who are the called according to his purpose. **-Romans 8:28**

Prayer

Father God, I trust You. My life is in Your hands. You are in control. Thank you for Your love, grace, and mercy. Thank You that I'm never alone on this journey. You lead me on a straight and purposeful path. I pray for wisdom, strength, and courage to be all You've created me to be and to follow You even when I don't see where the path is leading me. With love and gratitude, I commit my life and work to You. Thank You, God, for hearing and answering my prayer, in Jesus' name. Amen.

Storm Chaser

It has been said that you're either in a storm, heading to a storm, or coming out of one. Storms represent problems to which only the dead are exempt. Problems are a sign of life.

Every problem has a solution and possibly an advantage or lesson to be learned. During the storms of life, it's important to remember who you are in Christ and to know that He's at the Father's right hand, making intercession for you. Know that God cares about you and what you're going through. Know that He will see you through every storm of life.

To endure stormy weather, consider your perception of the situation. Measure your perception from these four angles:

1. The why
2. The how
3. Did you have the ability to prevent the matter?
4. Was it entirely out of your control?

You must be honest with yourself and take accountability. The storm must be embraced and diagnosed. When this is avoided, you push the life you were born to live farther away. Ask God for guidance and believe that He will be your refuge in any storm you face.

YOUR CHALLENGE

List at least three obstacles stopping you from achieving the life you were born to live.

1)____

____

____

2)____

____

____

3)____

____

____

Consider a different perception for each.

1)____

____

____

2)____

____

____

3)____

____

____

Today's Affirmation

God is in control.
(Romans 8:28)

Day 8

God's Word for You

Casting all your cares upon Him; for He careth for you.
- 1 Peter 5:7

Prayer

Father God, thank You for loving me unconditionally. Enable me to forgive myself and others as You've forgiven me. Thank You for tossing my sins and mistakes into the sea of forgetfulness. Please give me the hope and encouragement I need to overcome my mistakes. Help me press forward regardless of what it looks like, knowing that You are in control and I can live an abundant life because of Your sacrifice on Calvary. This is my prayer in Jesus' name. Amen.

Let it Go

How often do you lay awake, unable to sleep because past experiences are replaying in your mind, torturing you, and making you wish things were different?

Over the past seven days, you have been challenged to acknowledge your life's desires and identify what is holding you back. This is a significant step in the right direction. It's time to align your thoughts with your desires and allow God to order your steps. Our past affects our decisions, how we move, act, communicate, and even our health. To live our best life, we must eliminate past negativity and acknowledge that we are stronger, wiser, and better. Acknowledge your past, live in the present, and plan for the future. This is the challenge to define you and claim the promises of God with your name on them.

YOUR CHALLENGE

I challenge you to write a letter to your past. The purpose is to address why you aren't living the life God has for you. The letter should address any person or situation that continues to negatively occupy space in your head, where your fear is coming from, the obstacles you've faced, and why you've allowed these obstacles to hinder you. It's also a letter to yourself for forgiveness as you take lessons from the past to make a fresh start.

This letter symbolizes that you are "letting go." You are surrendering your life to God, and it is well with your soul.

You might say I've done that, and nothing happened. Ask yourself if you were sincere. Are you constantly looking back and turning your lessons into weapons instead of stepping stones?

These letters don't have to be shared with anyone unless necessary. If you're in a relationship or married, I double challenge you to complete a letter privately and together. A partnership such as marriage means two people become one, and what one feels affects the other. Tomorrow, you will release your letter to God, symbolizing your courage and willingness to start anew, to claim and manifest the life you were born to live. Believe in God and believe in yourself!

Today's Affirmation

I am a new creation in Christ.
The old has passed away.
(2 Corinthians 5:17)

Day 9

God's Word for You

Trust in the LORD with all thine heart; And lean not unto thine own understanding. In all thy ways acknowledge Him, And He shall direct thy paths. ***-Proverbs 3: 5-6***

Prayer

Father, thank You for another day. Please free me from doubt, self-will, pride, stubbornness, deception, dishonesty, and anything that's not like You. Help me recognize the opportunities and callings You have on my life. Illuminate the path You want me to walk. Fill me with strength and courage to pursue the mission You have set before me. Help me trust in Your timing and remain patient as Your plans unfold. May all I do and say bring You glory. This is my prayer in Jesus' name. Amen.

Welcome You

Today, you are officially giving your past to God. Look forward to something new, and when obstacles come, remember that they are only a piece of the puzzle. Connect them, learn from them, and grow with intention, knowing that you are walking in the direction ordained for you.

Let us pray with letters lifted towards Heaven and obstacles on your mind to release:

Father God, thank You for being the God of another chance. Thank You for picking me up and pulling me out of all my mistakes. Thank You for never giving up on me, even when I gave up on myself.

As I lift my letter to You, God, I ask that You remove every obstacle and forgive me for all the times I stepped outside Your will. Forgive me for not putting You first. Forgive me for my prideful ways. Forgive me for thinking I could ever do anything without You.

I come to You, Father because I need supernatural healing that only You can provide. I surrender all to You, Lord. Heal my broken heart and restore hope when I'm confused. Forgive me for trying to fix situations alone and being disobedient to Your voice. Forgive me for running in the opposite direction and looking for help when You were always there.

Thank You, Father, for guiding me through the difficult times. Thank You for being an ever-present help.

Thank You for Your grace and mercy. Thank You for Your power and presence. I love You, and I need You, Lord.

Father, You know my pain, my fears, and my burdens. I ask for Your healing and grace to cover every broken place. Heal every wound. Heal every heartache. Break every chain. Renew my mind to stay focused on Your direction to claim and manifest everything You have for me. Thank You, God! I know that You can do anything but fail.

Thank You for working everything together for my good. I release my past mistakes, cares, and life to You. I believe in Your goodness to see me through. Thank You for Your love and guidance. I'm claiming victory now! In Jesus' name, Amen.

Starting now, it's up to you! Will you move forward and claim the life God has waiting for you, or turn around to your past? I encourage you to live in the present and remember that God is in control. He loves you and wants the best for you!

YOUR CHALLENGE

Write one positive word that describes the new you.

I AM____

____

____

Note: Describe the new you with faith and action. Start looking forward and claiming only positive things. Your new self comes in a process; part one is being confident with who you are.

Today's Affirmation

I am healed in Jesus' name.
(Isaiah 53:5)

Day 10

God's Word for You

And be not conformed to this world: but be ye transformed by the renewing of your mind, that ye may prove what is that good, and acceptable, and perfect, will of God. For I say, through the grace given unto me, to every man that is among you, not to think of himself more highly than he ought to think, but to think soberly, according as God hath dealt to every man the measure of faith. **- Romans 12:2-3**

Prayer

Heavenly Father, our awesome God, thank You for all Your many blessings. If I had 10,000 tongues, I couldn't thank You enough. Thank You for allowing me to see a new day full of new mercies and opportunities. Forgive me, Father, for anything I've done or said that wasn't pleasing in Your sight. Draw me closer, Lord, so I may know and walk in Your ways. Give me a clean heart and renew the right spirit within me. I submit my will to Your will and thank You for the plans You have for me, the doors You've opened, and the ways You've made. I want to please You, God, and not people. This is my prayer in Jesus' name. Amen.

Why "Defining You" Is Necessary

Who am I? Am I living the life I desire or what others expect? Do physical possessions and accomplishments define me?

Defining You is about knowing you! What makes you smile, and what makes you anxious? It means identifying what's essential and what can wait until later. Identifying your strengths and weaknesses, behaviors, tendencies, and thought patterns is necessary to achieve your best life, the life God created you to live. God has a purpose and plan waiting for you to claim. If you can believe it, you can achieve it.

"Jesus said unto him, If thou canst believe, all things are possible to him that believeth." ***-Mark 9:23***

The process of Defining You can be compared to a two-edged sword. It may be scary as you uncover the layers of the current you, but it's therapeutic to discover who you are, what you want, and what you believe in. As you do the work, positives and negatives will be revealed, and you must change your perceptions. In reality, bad can be for your good, and sometimes good can distract you from your greatness. Defining You takes honesty, vulnerability, courage, and hard work.

Not defining yourself leads to a cycle of generational patterns. Not thinking for yourself and not being accountable for your choices because you're following learned behaviors without understanding the logic will hinder you from being all God created you to be.

"For we are his workmanship, created in Christ Jesus unto good works, which God hath before ordained that we should walk in them." ***- Ephesians 2:10***

Does the logic of "follow the leader, this is how I've always done things, or monkey see, monkey do" benefit your life? Often, this logic creates a closed-minded, stubborn attitude that delays living the life you were born to live. Solitude is the most incredible experience combined with meditation when Defining You. Be a lone wolf. Plan regular, consistent time and a designated place to spend with only God and you. Technology has its perks but should be limited to prevent distractions. Consider dedicating 30 minutes or more each day to focus on YOU!

Ask yourself the tough, soul-searching questions you would rather avoid and decide that only your opinion matters. Questions you might meditate on during your time in solitude include:

- Who am I?
- What do I want in life?
- What is the meaning of life?
- What is my true purpose?
- What is authentic within me?

- What does happiness mean to me?
- What would genuinely fulfill me?
- Is my attitude an obstacle?
- What legacy do I want to leave?

Meditating on these things is how you manifest the life you were born to live—the life of success, love, freedom, peace, and joy. Only you can DEFINE YOU, but honesty is required to claim and achieve your dreams. Start creating "Affirmation Statements" and read them daily as you define yourself. This type of statement is positive and used to help banish negative thoughts and accomplish goals. Affirmations are phrases repeated consistently aloud or to yourself to shift your mind toward peace, healing, joy, and positivity about yourself and your life. It's never too late to change your outlook on life. The more you repeat positive thoughts, the harder it is to remember the negative. Every morning, learn to start with a thankful heart and excitement about the blessings of a new day filled with new adventures and opportunities. Look at the bright side. Think, feel, believe, speak, and do only positive things. Nothing is impossible to those who believe!

YOUR CHALLENGE

Define **YOU** in one positive word:

I AM____

____

____

What are three things you are thankful for today?

1.____

____

____

2.____

____

____

3.____

____

____

Today's Affirmation

I am a living testimony of God's love and grace.
(John 3:16)

Day 11

God's Word for You

The tongue has the power of life and death, and those who love it will eat its fruit. **– Proverbs 18:21**

Prayer

Dear Heavenly Father: Thank You for blessing me to see a new day. I realize, God, that Your grace and mercy brought me this far. Thank You for loving me when I'm right and even when I'm wrong. Thank You for never giving up on me. I repent in Jesus' name and thank You for forgiving me. Help me, Father, to keep my mind focused on you, to make wise decisions, and to embrace the positive as You order my steps in Your Word. Help me be the light and salt You have called me to be so that I can be a blessing in the lives of others. I pray that You will renew my strength day by day. Please help me recognize the power in my thoughts and tongue and use it wisely. This is my prayer in Jesus' name. Amen.

I Am Who God Says I Am

The practice of positive thinking may take some time to cultivate, but it is achievable. Keep practicing.

One of the things I do is practice daily affirmations. Affirmations are positive phrases or sentences that motivate, inspire, and help us focus on our goals, which can help us change how we think, behave, and affect our environment. Words have power, but affirmations are ineffective if you don't believe what you're saying. There is no requirement for how long or short it should be. Write down what makes you happy. Recite it as often as possible until it's embedded in your mind, changing your thoughts. Remember, you are what you think!

Your Affirmation Blueprint

Follow these tips on writing affirmations:

1) Start with a repetitive statement like "I am."
2) Continue each "I am" statement so that they focus on what you want instead of what you're trying to avoid or eliminate from your life.

Example: Instead of writing, "I am going to be debt-free." Write the results of debt-free living: "I AM abundantly blessed!"

3) Write your affirmations in the present tense. Write as though you are experiencing what you want now.

Not "I am going to be a successful entrepreneur" but "I AM a successful entrepreneur."

"It's impossible" is a myth, not a fact. Nothing is impossible when you have faith in God and work towards your goals.

YOUR CHALLENGE

Define **YOU** in one positive word:

I AM____

____

____

What are you trusting God for right now?

I AM____

____

____

What transformation do you anticipate in your life?

I AM____

____

____

What is your boldest declaration for the future?

I AM____

____

____

Today's Affirmation

I am more than enough.
(2 Corinthians 12:9-10)

Day 12

God's Word for You

The counsel of the LORD standeth forever, the thoughts of his heart to all generations. **-Psalm 33:11**

Prayer

Dear God, thank You for allowing me to see another day. I ask You to forgive me for my sins. Strengthen me where I'm weak and build me up where I'm torn down. Search my heart and remove anything that's not like You. Allow me to hear Your voice and know right from wrong. Thank You for the patience, grace, love, and joy You have given me. Thank You for the calling You have on my life. Please help me be a good steward of every gift, talent, and opportunity You've given me. Help me learn to lean on Your ever-lasting arms, to know and do Your will. Thank You for drawing us closer to You and each other. This is my prayer in Jesus' name. Amen.

Friends or Frenemies

Talking about your plans creates an endorphin rush. The unconscious mind doesn't know the difference between imagined mental imagery versus actual, external reality. It thinks the topic of your conversation is real and rewards your brain chemistry accordingly. The cognitive process of visualizing future success convinces your unconscious mind that it's already happened. It doesn't fill your body with pre-victory anxiety. It fills it with a post-win celebration! Telling someone about your big idea is almost as emotionally rewarding as achieving it! And sharing your goals can put healthy pressure on you to reach them, but a word of caution here:

Sharing your dreams, goals, and plans with others isn't always the smartest thing to do. People may not always support your dreams. Some may be afraid, some are jealous, and some are just haters. Don't let negative energy from others defer your dreams or hold you back. So, be careful who you share your dreams with.

YOUR CHALLENGE

Define the word **GOAL:**

____

____

____

Write two sentences using the daily word to claim the life you were born to live.

1)______________________________________

____

____

____

2)______________________________________

____

____

____

Define **YOU** in one positive word:

I AM____________________________________

"For we are His workmanship, created in Christ Jesus unto good works, which God hath before ordained that we should walk in them." **- Ephesians 2:10**

Today's Affirmation

I have what it takes to succeed.
(Jeremiah 17:7)

Day 13

God's Word for You

Trust in the LORD with all your heart, And lean not on your own understanding; In all your ways acknowledge Him, And He shall direct your paths. **-Proverbs 3:5-6**

Prayer

Dear God, I thank You for this new day. I ask You to forgive my sins and strengthen me where I'm weak. Thank You in advance for Your peace, which surpasses all understanding. Thank You for working everything together for my good. Thank You for protecting me, my family, and my friends from dangers seen and unseen. Bless the work of my hands and allow it to be fruitful. I ask You to help control my tongue. Give me wisdom on when to speak, when to remain silent, what to say, and what not to say. Father, help me succeed in all I do for Your glory. Continue guiding me in the right direction. Grant me strength, patience, and wisdom to know and do Thy will. In the precious name of Jesus, I pray. Amen.

Mind Reset

To succeed at your life purpose, you must reset your mind and avoid unhealthy habits, relationships, and destructive cycles that hold you back. Immerse yourself in God's Word, pray for direction, follow His will for your life with persistence, and claim His promises with obedience, faith, and patience. Remember, God is in control, and He's never late. It will come to pass when He knows you can handle it with humility and appreciation. Don't let challenges and difficult situations discourage you. Every trial you face allows God to prove that you can depend on Him.

Journaling is a great way to reset your mind and improve your mental health. Writing skills or special equipment aren't required. Journaling can help your mental health by allowing you to examine patterns in your moods, reactions, behaviors, and thought processes. After understanding these patterns and triggers, it becomes possible to either alter them or modify how you react to them.

Have you ever said, "I don't know what to think or do?" Sometimes, there are so many ideas and options that it seems nearly impossible to sort through them. Writing is a way to eliminate many confusing thoughts and gain clarity. Journaling allows you to ask yourself questions about feelings, obstacles, and things you often neglect, such as "Are you making time for self-care?"

Journaling can become your method of coping with adverse situations. If you want to change your reality, you must change your subconscious thoughts and create a positive change toward a new reality that surpasses your imagination.

Your outer world is a reflection of your inner world. Something will manifest out of your thoughts; if negative thoughts creep into your mind, replace them immediately with positive thoughts. Remember that what you think about – you bring about. For instance, if your mind is overflowing with positive thoughts, you're more likely to attract positive experiences. On the other hand, if your subconscious thoughts are negative assumptions rooted in scarcity or negativity, these are the things you will most likely attract.

For as the body without the spirit is dead,
so faith without works is dead also.

- James 2:26

YOUR CHALLENGE

Define the word **SOLITUDE:**

____

____

____

Write two sentences describing the benefits of practicing solitude.

1)______________________________________

____

____

____

2)______________________________________

____

____

____

Define **YOU** in one positive word:

I AM____________________________________

Today's Affirmation

I serve a prayer-hearing and prayer-answering God.
(1 John 5:14-15)

Day 14

God's Word for You

Finally, brethren, whatsoever things are true, whatsoever things are honest, whatsoever things are just, whatsoever things are pure, whatsoever things are lovely, whatsoever things are of good report; if there be any virtue, and if there be any praise, think on these things.

- Philippians 4:8 (KJV)

Prayer

Lord Jesus, You are the way, the truth, and the life. I repent for my sins. Please continue to walk with me and hold my hand. Help me rise above life's storms and disasters by Your grace. Help me think right and be faithful to You for all the days of my life. Strengthen my good intentions. Renew my strength when I'm tired. Deliver me from anything that's not like You. Thank You for being my Lord and Savior. This is my prayer in Jesus' name. Amen.

Manifestation

Manifestation is turning your imagination into reality with actions of faith, prayer, and consistent work. It's a powerful tool for setting and accomplishing goals, and Defining You is the first step.

Manifestation is not solely based on your efforts but on the willingness to surrender to God's perfect plan and depend on Him for guidance.

"For I know the thoughts that I think toward you, saith the LORD, thoughts of peace, and not of evil, to give you an expected end." *- Jeremiah 29:11*

Manifestation isn't magic or an instant way to get whatever you want without dedication to the cause.

The Subconscious Mind

Have you ever wondered how your brain processes and stores all the experiences, emotions, habits, and memories that you accumulate over time? Well, the answer lies in your subconscious mind, which is like the basement of your brain. It's the part of your mind that operates whether you realize it or not. Think of it as a vast warehouse where everything important to you is kept safe and sound. The subconscious mind is the conductor of manifestation.

Your subconscious mind shapes your perceptions, emotions, actions, and life outcomes. When you respond to things without conscious thought, it indicates the influence of your subconscious mind, which directs most of your thoughts and behaviors, exerting significant influence over your life. So, if you ever feel stuck in a pattern or fall into the same situation, ask yourself:

What am I thinking?

Why am I thinking this?

Is this the action of my subconscious?

YOUR CHALLENGE

Define the word **PERCEPTION:**

____

____

____

Write two sentences using the daily word to claim the life you were born to live.

1)_______________________________________

____

____

____

2)_______________________________________

____

____

____

Define **YOU** in one positive word:

I AM___________________________________

Today's Affirmation

God is fighting my battles.
(Exodus 14:14)

Day 15

God's Word for You

To everything, there is a season and a time to every purpose under the heaven. ***-Ecclesiastes 3:1***

Prayer

Father God, this is the day that You have made. I will rejoice and be glad in it. How excellent is Your name in all the earth! There is power in Your name! You are the God that sees all and knows all. Help me, Father, to trust in Your timing. Help me remember that You are an on-time God. Forgive me, I pray, for all the times I failed to trust in Your timing. Forgive me when I ignored and disobeyed Your will and Your way. Help me to have faith and patience in knowing that You can do anything but fail. Help me let Your light shine through me while I wait. Grant me strength and courage to overcome every obstacle and wisdom to know that You don't make mistakes. Please bless, heal, and deliver all who pray this prayer in Jesus' name. Amen.

Is Manifestation Biblical?

The Bible does not discuss manifesting one's desires as commonly understood in modern spiritual practices based on the idea that you can think your dreams into reality. However, it does contain passages that encourage believers to have faith in God and trust in His plan for their lives. For instance, in **Mark 11:24**, Jesus says, *"Therefore I tell you, whatever you ask for in prayer, believe that you have received it, and it will be yours."* This passage suggests that faith plays a vital role in manifesting one's desires. In the biblical sense, this is what manifest means concerning reaching specific goals or outcomes. Notice the emphasis is on submitting to God's will and surrendering your desires to Him. The manifestation process in the Bible ultimately depends on God's will and His plan for an individual's life.

Once you confidently Define You through God's Word, you will only desire His will for your life. Your desires will align with what God has planned for you. You can ask Him for anything you want, but He will give you infinitely more than you can ever ask, think, or imagine, as stated in **Ephesians 3:20**.

God's riches, wisdom, and knowledge are unfathomable, and no one can understand His decisions and ways, as mentioned in **Romans 11:33**.

You must leave room for God's sovereignty to reign in your life and have faith in many possibilities. Still, ultimately, the sovereignty of God prevails over your beliefs and efforts. You should pray and let Him direct your life. This is how it should be: not asking for everything you want and expecting Him to fulfill every desire. Trust God to give you the life you were born to live!

YOUR CHALLENGE

Define the **SOVEREIGNTY OF GOD:**

____

____

____

Write two sentences using the daily word to claim the life you were born to live.

1)______________________________________

____

____

____

2)______________________________________

____

____

____

Define **YOU** in one positive word:

I AM___________________________________

Today's Affirmation

I am strong in the Lord and the power of His might.
(Ephesians 6:10)

Day 16

God's Word for You

Blessed is every one that feareth the LORD; that walketh in his ways. For thou shalt eat the labor of thine hands: happy shalt thou be, and it shall be well with thee.

- Psalm 128:1-2

Prayer

Lord God, I come to You with a grateful heart. You've been better to me than I've been to myself. Thank You for being the God of another chance. Help me to become more like You. Renew my mind and repair my body so I can continue to bring glory to Your name. By faith, I believe I can do everything according to Your will. Continue blessing and protecting me and Your people everywhere. Thank You for loving us unconditionally. I claim victory for the children of God, in Jesus' name. Amen.

Is Manifesting Dangerous?

Yes, manifesting (or the Law of Attraction) can be dangerous if it causes you to believe you can control everything in your life. God is the only one that has that power.

The Bible teaches us that the only manifestation is through the Holy Spirit for the common good. **1 Corinthians 12:7-8** says,

"To each is given the manifestation of the Holy Spirit for the common good. To one, there is given through the Spirit the message of wisdom; to another, the message of knowledge by means of the same Spirit; to another, faith by the same Spirit; to another, gifts of healing by that one Spirit. All of these are the work of one and the same Spirit, and he gives them to each one, just as he determines."

We can ask the Holy Spirit for things, but we must remember that when and how He gives them depends on God's will for our lives. We are not God and cannot manifest anything that is not in His will concerning us. We should rely on and trust God to provide and focus on gratitude. In **Philippians 4:6**, Paul encouraged us to be anxious for nothing. That doesn't mean we shouldn't be concerned. It means we should trust that God will work everything together for our good and be thankful. God loves and wants the best for His children. So, we have nothing to be afraid of or worry about. Put it in God's hands and leave it there.

We must also remember that when we desire something, we run the risk of that thing becoming an idol and replacing our focus on God. We should never put anything before God, not money, not people, nothing. **Colossians 2:8** says, *"See to it that no one takes you captive through hollow and deceptive philosophy, which depends on human tradition and the basic principles of this world rather than on Christ."*

All authority in heaven and on earth has been given to Jesus. If we have faith in Christ, we should not try to take authority from Him. We can work towards achieving anything we want, and if it is in God's plan for us, it will all come to fruition. Remember that God created the universe and created us to inhabit it. He has ultimate control, but He is a gracious and generous God and will provide all we need in His time. Trust God to do what is best for you. We should also ask the Holy Spirit to help us discern our wants from needs. We should ask for patience and guidance to have the wisdom and knowledge to make good decisions and take the right actions to produce results. Manifesting is not just about thinking correctly and producing the desires of your heart. God's Word is activated when we follow His word with faith and action. That is the prescription for manifesting the life you were born to live!

YOUR CHALLENGE

Define the word **ACTION**:

____

____

____

Write two sentences using the daily word to claim the life you were born to live.

1)______________________________________

____

____

____

2)______________________________________

____

____

____

Define **YOU** in one positive word:

I AM____________________________________

A man's heart plans his way,
But the Lord directs his steps. **- Proverbs 16:9**

Today's Affirmation

I am filled with hope and expectation.
(Psalm 62:5)

Day 17

God's Word for You

But they that wait upon the LORD shall renew their strength; they shall mount up with wings as eagles; they shall run, and not be weary; and they shall walk, and not faint. **-Isaiah 40:31**

Prayer

Father God, You are great and greatly to be praised. No one compares to You. Thank You for this new day and a new start. Lead me and guide me, I pray. Forgive me for my sins, mistakes, and failures. Give me a clean heart and renew my strength. Fill me with Your Holy Ghost's power to overcome every obstacle. Help me to know and show others that all things are possible with You, God, for those who believe! Give me direction to make better choices. Thank You for new opportunities to love, share, and be all You want me to be. In Jesus' name, I pray. Amen.

Faith, Fasting, Prayer, And Giving

If Jesus needed to fast for victory over Satan, it is a definite must for us, mere humans. In **Matt. 6:1-16**, Jesus talks about giving to those experiencing poverty, praying, and fasting as producing a reward. All three are to be done discreetly and from your heart. He promised to reward us openly when done this way. Over the next three days, we will explore understanding faith and how it works. Without faith and having a positive mindset, your luggage will roll on a continuous carousel, never to be claimed. The Bible defines faith as:

"The substance of things hoped for; the evidence of things not seen." **-Hebrews 11:1**

Faith is holding on to God's promises. Faith keeps you going when things are difficult, helps you see the positive in all things, boosts your mood, gives you courage, helps you discover your purpose, and enables you to be more productive and successful. Opportunities will pass us by without faith, but you must be willing to work hard, persevere, and never give up. The Bible says:

"Faith without works is dead." **-James 2:17**

Faith changes everything. This doesn't mean believing in God magically fixes everything around us. But faith changes our perspective so that we see things differently.

We can face significant difficulties with faith in God, knowing He will make a way and give us the strength to keep going.

There are three aspects of Faith:

1. In Whom do you believe?
2. What do you believe?
3. Why do you believe it?

We activate faith more than we realize daily. Faith is believing we will wake up in the morning. We have faith that the sun will rise and set each day. Faith is like accepting a person's word. Do you believe the Word of God?

To claim the life you were born to live requires determination and sacrifices. The question is: Do you believe in what you can't see? Are you willing to endure when things don't "seem" to go in your envisioned direction? Remember,

"All things are possible with God!"
- Matthew 19:26

YOUR CHALLENGE

Define the word **BELIEVE.**

____

____

____

Write two sentences using the daily word to claim the life you were born to live.

1)______________________________________

____

____

____

2)______________________________________

____

____

____

Define **YOU** in one positive word:

I AM___________________________________

Today's Affirmation

I am strong and determined.
(Ephesians 6:10)

Day 18

God's Word for You

And Jesus answering saith unto them,
Have faith in God. - **Mark 11:22**

Prayer

Heavenly Father, creator of every good and perfect gift, with outstretched hands, I ask You to forgive my sins and strengthen me where I'm weak. May Your peace fill my heart and mind as I release my cares and worries to You. Help me trust in Your plan for my life. Please grant me the strength and courage to face whatever comes my way with patience, grace, and calmness. I pray for peace in my relationships, home, community, and the world. Please give me the wisdom to make the right decisions and the boldness to carry them out. In Jesus' name, I pray. Amen.

Faith And Meditation

Hebrews 11:1 reads: "Now faith is the substance of things hope for, the evidence of things not seen."

This scripture speaks of having confidence and hope in the promises of God. It tells us to take God at His Word. He will never fail or go back on His Word because He is not a man that He should lie. You will find the wisdom necessary to accomplish God's will for your life through His Word. **Isaiah 26:23** says, *"You will keep in perfect peace those whose minds are steadfast because they trust in you."* To meditate means to think deeply in contemplation and reflection. Meditating on God's Word will permit it to be absorbed into your spirit, empowering you with the anointing to lift burdens and destroy yokes. You can overcome every adverse circumstance by getting the Word of God in your spirit and speaking the promises of God over your life. We must carefully consider what we believe and what our actions are. Without this introspection, we can neglect the importance of living righteously and following the lessons of the Bible.

The Bible teaches that we are justified by faith. That means we gain the right standing with our heavenly Father. God is no respecter of persons. What He's done for others – He will do for you. He said in **Malachi 3:6**, *"For I am the Lord, I change not...."*

Hebrews 11:6 says that without faith, it's impossible to please God. Put the law of faith into action by sowing the Word of God into your spirit, speaking it, and believing it. When God is pleased, He is moved to give you favor concerning what's going on in your life. His Word says that if you believe, you will receive (**Mark 11:24**).

YOUR CHALLENGE

Define the word **CLAIM**:

____

____

____

Write two sentences using the daily word to claim the life you were born to live.

1)_______________________________________

____

____

____

2)_______________________________________

____

____

____

Define **YOU** in one positive word:

I AM___________________________________

Today's Affirmation

I am accepted, anointed, and appointed.
(Ephesians 2:10)

Day 19

God's Word for You

And all things, whatsoever ye shall ask in prayer, believing, ye shall receive. **- Matthew 21:22**

Prayer

Father, thank You for Your grace and mercy. Thank You for loving me unconditionally. Forgive me for anything I've done or said against Your will. Thank You for Your unmerited favor in my life. Guide me in the path of love, kindness, and grace to be more like You. Continue watching over us, God. I pray for a special blessing for those struggling to know and do what's right. Lord, You know our strengths and weaknesses, and Your Word says when we're weak – You are strong. Thank You, God, for being an ever-present help and working everything together for our good. In Jesus' name and with thanksgiving, I pray. Amen.

Faith Is Power

Many believers never activate the anointing, power, and authority God has given them simply because they don't understand their covenant rights as children of God. Although they believe that the Holy Spirit inspired the writing of the Bible, they don't live by it. Many Christians allow obstacles to weaken their faith. In other words, they believe that God is all-powerful but lack the faith to believe in Him for deliverance from their negative circumstances.

Faith in God's Word gives you power over every circumstance and trial.

"For verily I say unto you, that whosoever shall say unto this mountain, Be thou removed, and be thou cast into the sea; and shall not doubt in his heart, but shall believe that those things which he saith shall come to pass; he shall have whatsoever he saith." - **Mark 11:23**

You can do the impossible by trusting in and relying on God's Word. According to **Jeremiah 33:3**, if you call on God, He promises to answer and show you great and mighty things. When your prayers align with God's Word, He will transform you with His supernatural power to destroy yolks and boldly claim what is yours. Look to Jesus, the author and finisher of our faith.

YOUR CHALLENGE

Define the word **ALIGN**:

____

____

____

Write two sentences using the daily word to claim the life you were born to live.

1)______________________________________

____

____

____

2)______________________________________

____

____

____

Define **YOU** in one positive word:

I AM___________________________________

Today's Affirmation

There is nothing too hard for God.
(Jeremiah 32:17)

Day 20

God's Word for You

If so be that ye have heard him, and have been taught by him, as the truth is in Jesus: That ye put off concerning the former conversation the old man, which is corrupt according to the deceitful lusts; And be renewed in the spirit of your mind; And that ye put on the new man, which after God is created in righteousness and true holiness. - **Ephesians 4: 21-24**

Prayer

Father God, I pray in Jesus' name that You will help me forget the things behind me so I can press toward the future You have for me. Restore me, Father, with Your grace and strength. Fill me with Your joy and peace. Help me to rely on You instead of my understanding. Remind me that Your thoughts and ways are higher than mine. Grant me peace, knowing I can do everything through Christ who strengthens me. In Jesus' name. Amen.

Giving

To expect and claim but not give isn't how life evolves. We often think of giving in terms of money; however, giving means much more. It means time, attention, compassion, presence, and wisdom, to name a few. Hoarding isn't a sign of expecting anything new. This behavior screams disbelief in better. If you are expecting more, make room for it! We're blessed to be a blessing. Giving is something every person can do, no matter your status. Helping others can help put things into perspective and make you feel more positive about your circumstances. Allow yourself time to unplug from the internet and explore the world. Social media has turned many of us into living, walking zombies. Research shows that giving boosts our overall well-being and lessens depression. Your giving will lead to a life of generosity and abundance. Look around you, count your blessings, and do good for others. Pay for someone's coffee, sit with someone lonely, ask someone about their day, and pray for more ways to give.

"Be not deceived; God is not mocked: for whatsoever a man soweth, that shall he also reap." **-Galatians 6:7**

YOUR CHALLENGE

Define the word **GENEROSITY**:

____

____

____

Write two sentences using the daily word to claim the life you were born to live.

1)______________________________________

____

____

____

2)______________________________________

____

____

____

Define **YOU** in one positive word:

I AM___________________________________

Today's Affirmation

I'm blessed to be a blessing.
(Luke 6:38)

Day 21

God's Word for You

For the LORD God is a sun and shield: the LORD will give grace and glory: no good thing will he withhold from them that walk uprightly. **- Psalm 84:11**

Prayer

Father God, Your Word reminds us that weeping may endure for a night, but joy comes in the morning. Thank You for this new day. I will rejoice and be glad in it! I pray for strength that only You can provide. Allow me to walk in faith and love. Make me an overcomer, and fill me with Your wisdom. Father, this is my prayer in Jesus' name. Amen.

The Power of Prayer

We serve a prayer hearing and prayer answering God, who tells us to put everything in His hands. It doesn't take a lot of fancy words; pray with a humble heart in faith, knowing that our God knows us fully and completely.

1 Thessalonians 5:17-18 tells us to *"pray without ceasing, give thanks in all circumstances; for this is the will of God in Christ Jesus for you."* What does that mean?

It means having a prayerful attitude, knowing that the Holy Spirit dwells within us and that we can call on God at any time of day or night. It means constant communion with Him - praying about everything and worrying about nothing. Our circumstances and who we become greatly depend on our prayer life. Consistency equals stability, strength, and power.

"Create a clean heart, O God, and renew a right spirit within me." ***- Psalm 51:10***

Prayer is a conversation between you and God. During prayer, you humbly communicate with Him to confess your sins, seek forgiveness, give thanks, and ask for whatever you desire.

Prayer is always the answer, but faith unlocks the door. God has a great plan waiting for you. Claim it by faith. Fear is the opposite of faith. And remember, prayer is a two-way conversation. You have to listen as well as pray.

We are also encouraged to give thanks in all circumstances. We do so in God's will because no matter how difficult life gets, there is always something to be thankful for. We know that our trials come to make us strong, His grace is sufficient, and He will work everything together for our good.

YOUR CHALLENGE

Define the word **PERSISTENCE**:

____

____

____

Write two sentences using the daily word to claim the life you were born to live.

1)______________________________________

____

____

____

2)______________________________________

____

____

____

Define **YOU** in one positive word:

I AM____________________________________

Today's Affirmation

I am chosen.
(John 15:16)

Day 22

God's Word for You

Neither is there any creature that is not manifest in his sight: but all things are naked and opened unto the eyes of him with whom we have to do. Seeing then that we have a great high priest that is passed into the heavens, Jesus the Son of God, let us hold fast our profession. For we have not a high priest which cannot be touched with the feeling of our infirmities; but was in all points tempted like as we are, yet without sin. Let us therefore come boldly unto the throne of grace, that we may obtain mercy, and find grace to help in time of need.

- Hebrews 4:13-16

Prayer

Father God, I'm coming to You now to thank You for last night's sleep and rest. Thank You for keeping me all down through the years and never leaving me. I pray that You will forgive me for my sins and give me the grace to forgive others. And Father, I pray for all who need healing and restoration of their body, mind, soul, and spirit. Allow them to feel Your love wherever they are. God, You are excellent in all Your ways. No one compares to You. You're God all by Yourself! Continue wrapping Your arms of protection around us, fill us with Your love, and guide us day by day.

Thank You! Thank You! Thank You God! In Jesus' name, I pray. Amen.

The Prayer of Jabez- Introduction

The Prayer of Jabez is a one-sentence prayer found in **1 Chronicles 4:10**. It's a prayer by a man named "Jabez," who asked for a blessing, which God granted.

"And Jabez called on the God of Israel, saying, Oh that thou wouldest bless me indeed, and enlarge my coast, and that thine hand might be with me, and that thou wouldest keep me from evil, that it may not grieve me! And God granted him that which he requested."

–1 Chronicles 4:10

Jabez's prayer seeks God's favor, guidance, and protection. It also reflects a heartfelt plea for a closer relationship with God and personal spiritual growth. It encourages us to acknowledge God's sovereignty and align our desires with His will. Jabez's prayer expresses faith and trust in God and seeks His blessings and guidance in all aspects of life. It encapsulates the desire for genuine prosperity, spiritual abundance, and personal growth.

The name Jabez is of Hebrew origin. The meaning of Jabez is "he makes sorrowful." His mother named him this because bearing him during childbirth caused her extreme pain. Jabez was an ordinary man who believed in God and wanted more for his life than his name implied. This prayer encompasses four core elements:

1. **Blessing**: Oh, that you would bless me.
2. **Enlargement**: Enlarge my territory.
3. **Guidance**: Let your hand be with me.
4. **Protection**: Keep me from harm and free of pain.

Applying this prayer to your life is a desire to pursue the most prosperous life possible without limits by faith. Over the next four days, we will explore the Prayer of Jabez and how to add it to your life to manifest what God has waiting for you to claim!

YOUR CHALLENGE

Define the word **ACCOUNTABILITY**:

____

____

____

Write two sentences using the daily word to claim the life you were born to live.

1)____

____

____

____

2)____

____

____

____

Define **YOU** in one positive word:

I AM____

Today's Affirmation

God is working everything together for my good.
(Romans 8:28)

Day 23

God's Word for You

He that hath no rule over his own spirit is like a city that is broken down and without walls. - **Proverbs 25:28**

Prayer

Almighty God, in whom we live, move, and have our being. Thank You for last night's sleep and rest and for allowing us to see another day. Thank You for loving us unconditionally. Thank You for Your grace and mercy. Thank You for Jesus, our wonderful Savior, and the Holy Spirit, who leads, guides, comforts, and teaches. I pray for a fresh anointing and the fruit of the Spirit: love, joy, peace, patience, kindness, goodness, faithfulness, gentleness, and self-control.

Please, Father, forgive me for anything I've done that wasn't pleasing in Your sight. I pray that you will help me to be a better person. Heal my heart, guide my feet, and keep Your arms of protection around me.

I pray that those who don't know You will come asking, "What must I do to be saved?" Give us wisdom and a heart to share the gospel throughout the world. Help us remember that You are in control and can do anything but fail. Thank You for being the great God that You are. By faith, in Jesus' name, I pray. Amen.

The Prayer of Jabez (Part 1)

"Oh, That you would bless me."

Jabez boldly believed that his faith in God was the reason for all the joy in his life. He knew the Lord was the source of all blessings and asked to be blessed. These blessings are material, like money and success. They're also spiritual, like good relationships with others, peace of mind, a quiet and gentle spirit, and a compassionate heart. When we pray to God, He blesses us both spiritually and materially. So, remember that prayer still works the next time you feel your prayers have gone unanswered. God always answers us, maybe not in the time frame or the way we had hoped, but He does answer us, and often in a way more incredible than we could have ever imagined!

Even the person with the most seemingly perfect life has difficult circumstances despite what you see on social media. There is no such thing as a trouble-free life, and God never promised that there would be, but He is a loving Father who provides for His children. Christ warned us about the difficulties we face in this world and told his followers to expect trials from time to time **(John 16:33)** but remember, our trials come to make us strong. **Genesis 22:14** reminds us that God is **Jehovah Jireh**, the Hebrew word translated as "the LORD will provide." We must remember that He answers prayers according to His will, not ours. If you knew that something you desired would create a tornado, wouldn't you want to be warned or stopped in your tracks? Trust God in every situation, and you will manifest the life you were born to live!

YOUR CHALLENGE

Define the word **BOLD**:

____

____

____

Write two sentences using the daily word to claim the life you were born to live.

1)____

____

____

____

2)____

____

____

____

Define **YOU** in one positive word:

I AM____

Today's Affirmation

I am strong in the Lord and the power of His might.
(Ephesians 6:10)

Day 24

God's Word for You

Do not be anxious about anything, but in everything, by prayer and supplication with thanksgiving, let your requests be made known to God. – **Philippians 4:6**

Prayer

Father God, Awesome Ruler, Creator of the Universe: My heart is full of gratitude and praise! Thank You, Father, for Your abundant blessings. Thank You for being a prayer-hearing and prayer-answering God. Thank You for looking beyond my faults and seeing my needs. Thank You for never leaving or forsaking us. There is no one like You, Mighty God, Wonderful Counselor! Everlasting Father, Prince of Peace! From the rising of the sun to the going down of the same, You are worthy to be praised! Thank You for life, health, and strength. Thank You for saving me. Thank You for keeping me through the tough times.

Forgive me, Father, for my faults and sins. Guide me, Lord, to live a better life today and every day. Grant me the spirit of discernment that I will know right from wrong. Increase my faith so I can move mountains and give me divine protection. May Your light shine brighter in me each day so that I might follow the path of righteousness and be a blessing to others. Father, this is my prayer in Jesus' name. Amen.

The Prayer of Jabez (Part 2)

"And enlarge my border."

Jabez's intentions focused not on physical territory but on impacting God's kingdom. His desire had nothing to do with land at all. When we analyze the spiritual meaning of this line, we can see that it is different from what we might initially think. Jabez wanted to influence those around him positively, and he devoted time to praying that God would expand the boundaries of his heart so it could overflow. He wished to transform the lives of others for God's Kingdom, which is not a selfish prayer. Jabez had a strong desire to serve God.

YOUR CHALLENGE

Define the word **CONFIDENT**:

____

____

____

Write two sentences using the daily word to claim the life you were born to live.

1)____

____

____

____

2)____

____

____

____

Define **YOU** in one positive word:

I AM______________________________________

Today's Affirmation

My ministry is blessed and fruitful.
(Jeremiah 17:7-8)

Day 25

God's Word for You

Therefore, I say unto you, What things soever ye desire when ye pray, believe that ye receive them, and ye shall have them. **-Mark 11:24**

Prayer

Dear God, thank You for this beautiful sunrise. Thank You for waking me up this morning with a reasonable portion of my health and strength. Thank You for keeping me in my right mind. Thank You for blessings that I don't even deserve. Forgive me, Father, for my sins, and give me grace to forgive others. Quiet my heart, give rest to my soul, and refocus my spirit—for true renewal comes only from You. Help me, Lord, to be intentional with my time and worship. Prepare my mind and body for the days to come, and send Your healing power to those in need. I thank You in Jesus' name for these and all other blessings. Amen.

The Prayer of Jabez (Part 3)

"and that your hand might be with me."

Jabez recognized that he had limitations as a person. To be effective in ministry and life, he needed God's help. Jabez believed God was all-powerful and asked for guidance and protection to stay on the right path. Most importantly, he asked to be held close by God's embrace. He understood that all his help and blessings came from God, without whom he could do nothing.

YOUR CHALLENGE

Define the word **ACKNOWLEDGE**:

____

____

____

Write two sentences using the daily word to claim the life you were born to live.

1)______________________________________

____

____

____

2)______________________________________

____

____

____

Define **YOU** in one positive word:

I AM____________________________________

Today's Affirmation

I am created in Christ to do good works.
(Ephesians 2:10)

Day 26

God's Word for You

Be strong and of a good courage, fear not, nor be afraid of them: for the LORD thy God, he it is that doth go with thee; he will not fail thee, nor forsake thee.

- Deuteronomy 31:6

Prayer

Father, I bow before You now to thank You for all your many blessings. Thank You for last night's sleep and rest. Thank You for keeping your loving arms of protection around me. Thank You for keeping me in my right mind. Thank You for being my strength and refuge, a very present help in times of trouble. I confess that I've done wrong and ask You to forgive me for all the times I fell short of Your glory. I pray that You will meet every need and bless Your children worldwide. I praise Your name today because You're worthy to be praised. Thank You, Father, that no weapon formed against me will prosper. In Jesus' name, I pray. Amen.

The Prayer of Jabez (Part 4)

"and that you would keep me from harm so that it might not bring me pain."

Jabez, which means "he causes pain" in Hebrew, renounced the sorrowful meaning of his name through prayer. He prayed to be protected from harm, just as Jesus taught His disciples to pray. Jabez had confidence in God as his defender. Jabez's prayer is powerful and can transform lives and communities. Surrendering to God's will and incorporating the principles of the Jabez Prayer into our lives will unlock a deeper faith and abundant blessings that flow from a close relationship with God. It teaches us the importance of trusting God's plan and seeking His guidance.

YOUR CHALLENGE

Define the word **CONFIDENT**:

____

____

____

Write two sentences using the daily word to claim the life you were born to live.

1)______________________________________

____

____

____

2)______________________________________

____

____

____

Define **YOU** in one positive word:

I AM___________________________________

Today's Affirmation

I am a child of God and a co-heir with Christ.
(Romans 8:16-17)

Day 27

God's Word for You

For I know the thoughts that I think toward you, saith the LORD, thoughts of peace, and not of evil, to give you an expected end. –**Jeremiah 29:11**

Prayer

Heavenly Father, I come before Your throne of grace, acknowledging Your sovereignty and lovingkindness. You are the source of every good and perfect gift, and I am eternally grateful for Your unwavering love and care. Forgive us, Lord, for our shortcomings and failures. Create in us a clean heart and a renewed spirit so that we might walk in righteousness and bring glory to Your holy name. Strengthen our faith and fill us with Your peace. Help us to live in unity and harmony, loving one another as You have loved us. Equip us with the strength to overcome adversity and to persevere in Your ways. In Jesus' name, I pray, with thanksgiving, Amen.

A Prayer of Petition

A petition is a formal written request to an authority or organized body, such as a court. It can also be a written request or call for change signed by many people to support a shared cause or concern or an earnest request in general. In a religious context, a petition asks God for something through a formal prayer. We ask the Lord for various things, such as wisdom, guidance, healing, providence, and protection, while kneeling and surrendering our souls. A prayer of petition is any prayer that asks God for something. When we ask for wisdom, direction, healing, or other things, we pray prayers of petition. For instance, Jabez's prayer to God to enlarge his territory was a prayer of petition. The Bible contains petition prayers where people ask for something on their behalf or for others. Our Heavenly Father loves us and hears our prayers. It is natural for us to seek guidance and help from our creator.

Petition God for Comfort When You Feel Disconnected

At that time, Jesus answered and said, I thank thee, O Father, Lord of heaven and earth, because thou hast hid these things from the wise and prudent, and hast revealed them unto babes. Even so, Father: for so it seemed good in thy sight. All things are delivered unto me of my Father: and no man knoweth the Son, but the Father; neither knoweth any man the Father, save the Son, and he to whomsoever the Son will reveal him. Come unto me, all ye that labor and are heavy laden, and I will give you rest. Take my yoke upon you, and learn of me; for I am meek and lowly in heart: and ye shall find rest unto your souls. For my yoke is easy, and my burden is light. ***– Matthew 11:25-30***

Petition God for Hope When You Feel Hopeless

"Now the God of hope fill you with all joy and peace in believing, that ye may abound in hope through the power of the Holy Ghost." **– Romans 15:13**

To pray like Jabez, follow these three steps:

1. Pray with the right attitude, including an earnest and repentant heart seeking God. Jesus taught us how to pray in **Matthew 6:5-15**: simple, direct, and sincere.

2. Submit to the power and leading of the Holy Spirit, who will guide you in how to pray. As **Romans 8:26-27** reminds us,

"The Spirit helps us in our weakness. We do not know what we ought to pray for, but the Spirit himself intercedes for us through wordless groans. And he who searches our hearts knows the mind of the Spirit because the Spirit intercedes for God's people following the will of God."

3. Pray in the name of Jesus. As Peter explained in **Acts 3:16**:

"By faith in the name of Jesus, this man whom you see and know was made strong. Jesus' name and the faith that comes through him have completely healed him, as you can all see."

As you deepen your understanding of God's Word, you will realize that Jesus used Scripture to resist Satan. When we incorporate the Word of God into our prayers of petition, its living and active power becomes visible. Therefore, start claiming what is rightfully yours by approaching God in prayer.

YOUR CHALLENGE

Define the word **PETITION**:

____

____

____

Write two sentences using the daily word to claim the life you were born to live.

1)______________________________________

____

____

____

2)______________________________________

____

____

____

Define **YOU** in one positive word:

I AM___________________________________

Today's Affirmation

I am growing in grace and holiness
by the power of the Holy Spirit.
(2 Peter 3:18)

Day 28

God's Word for You

This book of the law shall not depart out of thy mouth, but thou shalt meditate therein day and night, that thou mayest observe to do according to all that is written therein: for then thou shalt make thy way prosperous, and then thou shalt have good success.

- Joshua 1:8

Prayer

Father God, thank You that Your grace is sufficient and Your power is made perfect in our weakness. We thank You, God, for being a healer who can meet every need. Your Word says, "Commit to the Lord whatever you do, and He will establish Your plans." I desire to follow You, God.

Today, I put it all in Your hands. Enable me to use the gifts, talents, and abilities You've entrusted to me so that I might be a light in the darkness. Remove anything that's not like you in my life; anything weighing me down, anything that gives me anxiety, anything that's toxic. Give me the power to resist temptation and boldness to tell Satan "No." Grant me wisdom to know what's good and bad for me and strength to keep the devil under my feet. I praise and honor you, God, and believe all these things are done in the mighty and matchless name of Jesus Christ. Amen!

Fasting

Fasting is voluntarily abstaining from food or other pleasures for a specified period to concentrate on you and your higher power. This action demonstrates the urgency to claim your desires, the discipline of self-control, and tunes our antennas toward God.

Self-discipline is necessary to overcome obstacles. It's the ability to stay motivated and act regardless of your feelings. Research shows that self-discipline is a more accurate predictor of success than a person's IQ. It's like a muscle; the more you work or practice, the stronger you will become.

Fasting and prayer align us with the purpose God has for us. However, it should never be pursued as an act of manipulating or forcing God into action. God answers according to His will.

I challenge you to plan a five-day fast starting on Day 31. Why not? Are you ready to claim what God has for you, the direction to take, and peace that surpasses understanding? For the remainder of this day, meditate on your heart's desire and EXPECT to hear a clear voice from Heaven.

Tomorrow is planning day!

YOUR CHALLENGE

Define the word **ABSTAIN**:

____

____

____

Write two sentences using the daily word to claim the life you were born to live.

1)______________________________________

____

____

____

2)______________________________________

____

____

____

Define **YOU** in one positive word:

I AM____________________________________

Today's Affirmation

"God is always with me."
(Matthew 28:20)

Day 29

God's Word for You

The preparations of the heart in man, and the answer of the tongue, is from the LORD. All the ways of a man are clean in his own eyes, but the LORD weigheth the spirits. Commit thy works unto the LORD, and thy thoughts shall be established. The LORD hath made all things for himself: yea, even the wicked for the day of evil. Everyone that is proud in heart is an abomination to the LORD: though hand join in hand, he shall not be unpunished. By mercy and truth, iniquity is purged: and by the fear of the LORD, men depart from evil. When a man's ways please the LORD, he maketh even his enemies to be at peace with him. Better is a little with righteousness than great revenues without right. A man's heart deviseth his way: but the LORD directeth his steps. **–Proverbs 16:1–9**

Prayer

Almighty God, I praise Your name today because You've been better to us than we've been to ourselves. Thank You, God, for blessing us over, above, and beyond all we could ever hope, ask, think, or pray for. If we had ten thousand tongues, we couldn't praise You enough. Every day is a gift from You, God; without You, we would have nothing. Grant us wisdom and humility, Father, to remember where all our blessings come from. Help us know that all things are possible with You, but we can do nothing without You. Continue to order our steps, Lord, in Jesus' holy name. Amen.

Fasting Mistakes

In the Bible, in **Matthew 6:16-18**, Jesus teaches His followers not to be like hypocrites when they perform acts of devotion such as giving to the needy, praying, and fasting. He warns them not to do these things to be praised by people but rather for God. When fasting and praying, Jesus says that they should not be done to be seen by others but rather in secret, where only God can see them.

However, this does not mean it is wrong for people to see that you are fasting and praying. If someone asks you why you are not eating, it is better to be honest and tell them you are fasting. You do not have to make a big deal out of it, but you should be truthful. If they have further questions, answer them in a way that glorifies God rather than exalting yourself for your acts of faith. It is crucial to avoid being legalistic about your acts of devotion. Jesus did not say you broke your fast if you told someone you were fasting. The spirit of the fast is broken when you are more concerned about keeping it a secret from others than feeding your hunger for God by abstaining from food for a reason. In all that you do, whether you eat or drink or whatever else, do it to the glory of God, as **1 Corinthians 10:31** teaches us. Focus on claiming and manifesting the life you were born to live!

YOUR CHALLENGE

Define the word **ENVISION**:

____

____

____

Write two sentences using the daily word to claim the life you were born to live.

1)______________________________________

____

____

2)______________________________________

____

____

Define **YOU** in one positive word:

I AM____________________________________

Today's Affirmation

I am who God says I am.
(Deuteronomy 28:13)

Day 30

God's Word for You

Moreover, when ye fast, be not, as the hypocrites, of a sad countenance: for they disfigure their faces, that they may appear unto men too fast. Verily I say unto you, They have their reward. But thou, when thou fastest, anoint thine head, and wash thy face; That thou appear not unto men to fast, but unto thy Father which is in secret: and thy Father, which seeth in secret, shall reward thee openly.

- Matthew 6:16-18 (KJV)

Prayer

Almighty God, my Father, thank You for the blessing of another day. Thank You for Your grace and mercy. Thank You for Your love, peace, and joy. Thank You for Your promise never to leave or forsake me. Thank You, God, that I can run to You when times get hard. Forgive me for my sins as I forgive those who have sinned against me. Protect me from all that is evil. Remove anything in me that's not like You. Heal my mind, body, soul, and spirit so that I may bring them under subjection to You. Loosen the chains that bind me and strengthen me where I'm weak for Your glory. In Jesus' mighty name, I pray. Amen.

Let's Plan

Planning is required to achieve any goal, but we must take one step at a time. Multi-tasking is excellent but can lead to burnout, which depletes your reward once it's achieved. As you plan your "fasting and prayer week," ask God for peace, guidance, and strength. Take time to read God's Word, journal, and be consistent! The Bible tells us that fasting intensifies prayer. **Psalm 23** tells us that God is with us through everything. He is there to comfort, help, and guide us through our trials and tribulations. Whenever you start feeling anxious, overwhelmed, or discouraged, recite and remember the following:

"The LORD is my shepherd; I shall not want. He maketh me to lie down in green pastures: he leadeth me beside the still waters. He restoreth my soul: he leadeth me in the paths of righteousness for his name's sake. Yea, though I walk through the valley of the shadow of death, I will fear no evil: for thou art with me; thy rod and thy staff they comfort me. Thou preparest a table before me in the presence of mine enemies: thou anointest my head with oil; my cup runneth over. Surely goodness and mercy shall follow me all the days of my life: and I will dwell in the house of the LORD forever." ***- Psalm 23***

YOUR CHALLENGE

Define the word **DISCIPLINE**:

___

___

___

Write two sentences using the daily word to claim the life you were born to live.

1)___

___

___

2)___

___

___

What will I fast from; "give up?" Food, screen time, bad habits, gossiping, excessive shopping, entertainment, personal comfort, etc. (something that would be a real sacrifice for you.)

___

___

___

What time will I fast, pray, and seek God daily?

____

____

____

What would I like to focus on in prayer during that time?

1)______________________________________

____

____

2)______________________________________

____

____

Define **YOU** in one positive word:

I AM___________________________________

Today's Affirmation

Nothing can separate me from the love of God.
(Romans 8:38-39)

Day 31

God's Word for You

And let us not be weary in well doing: for in due season we shall reap, if we faint not. - **Galatians 6:9**

Prayer

Dear Heavenly Father: I humble myself before You now, asking that You forgive me for my sins and give me the grace to forgive others. I pray for wisdom and guidance to fulfill Your purpose for my life. I claim everything You have for me in Jesus' name. Not my will, but Thy will be done. Thank You for loving me unconditionally. Thank You for keeping me and never giving up on me. I pray that You will continue to shape me in Your image and keep Your loving arms around me. Please give me the strength to endure and hope to persevere. I count it all done in Jesus' name. Amen.

Fasting & Prayer (Day 1 Of 5)

SAY "THANK YOU"

Have you ever felt that you deserved a "thank you" but didn't receive one? How does receiving a "thank you" make you feel?

Contrary to some myths, life wasn't created by chance. It's a divine creation that only God can do. No matter how much science evolves, nothing can be replicated without God as the foundation. As you begin and continue your fast, pay attention to life - the air, water, insects, weather, and everything else in your surroundings. Consider what you take for granted and how life would change with one missing link. This small but powerful phrase acknowledges every moment, encounter, and breath as a gift. Saying THANK YOU fertilizes your "manifestation ability seeds" to grow beyond imagination.

Saying "thank you" is a form of prayer when your heart is in the right place and focused on our Heavenly Father, Creator of the universe.

Remember, empty words, fancy quotes, or theatrics don't move God. A meaningful Thank You creates space for miracles and the revelation of God's plan. Manifestation happens from a grateful and sincere heart. "Thank You" makes room for more!

YOUR CHALLENGE

Define the word **GRATITUDE**:

____

____

____

Write two sentences using the daily word to claim the life you were born to live.

1)______________________________________

____

____

2)______________________________________

____

____

Define **YOU** in one positive word:

I AM____________________________________

Today's Affirmation

I am blessed, highly favored, and thankful!
(Psalm 90:17)

Day 32

God's Word for You

Be strong and of a good courage, fear not, nor be afraid of them: for the LORD thy God, he it is that doth go with thee; he will not fail thee, nor forsake thee.

- Deuteronomy 31:6

Prayer

Father God, I praise Your name because You are worthy to be praised. Thank You for allowing us to see each other another day. You didn't have to do it, but You did. Today, I pray for those standing in need. I lift before You those who don't know You in the pardon of their sins. Father, have Your way. Provide comfort, healing, salvation, and deliverance. Give Your angels charge over us. May Your Word be a lamp unto our feet and a light unto our path. Help us remember that there is nothing too hard for You. We can do all things through Christ, who strengthens us. Grant us favor and success. Thank You, God, in Jesus' name. Amen.

Fasting & Prayer (Day 2)

Give By Faith and Continue Moving Forward

Giving is an act of worship that pleases God when we live by faith. It spreads His love and serves as a way to express gratitude to Him. Giving can take many forms, including emotional, physical, mental, and spiritual. You can help animals, "God's Creation," strangers, "God's Creation," and even the environment you live in "God's Creation." Teach a skill someone blessed you to learn, sit with someone alone and be a listening ear, visit the sick and shut-in whether you know them personally or not, lend a helping hand unselfishly "not looking for anything in return," volunteer in your community, and whatever God leads you to do for His glory.

"Whatsoever thy hand findeth to do, do it with thy might; for there is no work, nor device, nor knowledge, nor wisdom, in the grave, whither thou goest."

- Ecclesiastes 9:10

Giving aligns with Jesus' example and is a testament to the gospel. Jesus came to earth *"not to be served, but to serve, and to give His life as a ransom for many"* **(Matthew 20:28)**.

In the act of giving, we mirror the essence of Christ and embody the gospel through the use of our resources. Generosity is not just a virtue but a calling for Christians, echoing our devotion to a God whose very nature is sacrificial giving **(John 3:16)**. We step beyond ourselves and serve others when we give our money, time, talents, and gifts. Giving cultivates virtues such as compassion, kindness, joy, and love.

Generosity not only enriches others but cultivates contentment within ourselves. By freely sharing our resources, we celebrate God's abundant blessings and recognize Him as our ultimate source of provision. While receiving is a joy, the most authentic fulfillment lies in the joy of giving. Scripture warns against the love of money, calling it the root of all evil **(1 Timothy 6:10). Ecclesiastes 5:10** emphasizes the futility of loving money by stating, *"Whoever loves money never has enough; whoever loves wealth is never satisfied with their income."* We combat greediness by freely giving to those in need.

"Give, and it shall be given unto you; good measure, pressed down, and shaken together, and running over, shall men give into your bosom. For with the same measure that ye mete withal, it shall be measured to you again." **-Luke 6:38**

Add giving with gratitude, faith, and prayer to your lifestyle to claim and manifest the life you were born to live!

YOUR CHALLENGE

Define the word **COURAGE**:

____

____

____

Write two sentences using the daily word to claim the life you were born to live.

1)______________________________________

____

____

2)______________________________________

____

____

Define **YOU** in one positive word:

I AM____________________________________

Today's Affirmation

I am strong and courageous in the Lord.
(Joshua 1:9)

Day 33

God's Word for You

Be very careful, then, how you live--not as unwise but as wise, making the most of every opportunity because the days are evil. Therefore, do not be foolish, but understand what the Lord's will is. **-Ephesians 5:15-17**

Prayer

Our Father and our God, in whom we live, move, and have our being. This is the day that You have made. I will rejoice and be glad in it! Thank You for being the God of another chance. Thank You for forgiving my sins and never giving up on me. Your Word says in **Jeremiah 29:11**, *"For I know the plans I have for you, declares the LORD, plans to prosper you and not to harm you, plans to give you hope and a future."* I believe You have an excellent plan for me, and I ask You to provide me with faith and boldness to be all You created and called me to be.

Elevate my mind. Help me grow in grace and knowledge. May the joy of the Lord be my strength. Grant me peace and wisdom to ignore the enemy's distractions. Bless humanity everywhere. By faith, I claim every promise is true and count it all done. In Jesus' name, I pray. Amen.

Fasting & Prayer (Day 3)

Conquer Your Fear

Fear is a common emotion that everyone processes differently. Being afraid becomes an excuse; not trying means defeat.

"For we walk by faith, not by sight."
-2 Corinthians 5:7

We were designed to be strong by believing in God and ourselves. With these elements, the word "CAN'T" should be limited in your daily vocabulary, and "CAN" should be used in every obstacle. Never think of yourself failing, which leads to failure. Whenever negative thoughts surface, quickly cancel them with positive thoughts.

If you were to think about every goal you have accomplished, every obstacle you have overcome, and every time someone mentioned what you couldn't do but achieved success, you would surprise yourself. Yes, you did it, and you can do it again. When you focus on fear, that is what you will manifest. Look at the world's many wonders and discover how ordinary individuals' visions, once considered impossible, became possible.

As you continue your fast with faith, cast your fears onto God to claim and manifest the life you were born to live!

YOUR CHALLENGE

Define the word **WISDOM**:

____

____

____

Write two sentences using the daily word to claim the life you were born to live.

1)______________________________________

____

____

2)______________________________________

____

____

Define **YOU** in one positive word:

I AM___________________________________

Today's Affirmation

I am in God's hand.
(Isaiah 41:13)

Day 34

God's Word for You

Trust in the LORD with all thine heart; and lean not unto thine own understanding. In all thy ways acknowledge him, and he shall direct thy paths. - **Proverbs 3:5-6**

Prayer

Father God, I've come to say thank You for how You've blessed and kept me every day of my life. Most of all, thank You for Your Son Jesus and the gift of the Holy Spirit. My heart is happy, and I rejoice in knowing that all of our help comes from You, that You're always on time, and that You never fail. Today, I lift all humanity before You. Help us to lean on You instead of our imperfect understanding. Help us to know that You care. Help us to trust You with our decisions. Help us know that you're in control. Thank You for Your Spirit to comfort us and Your wisdom to guide us. Father, this is my prayer in Jesus' name. Amen.

Fasting & Prayer (Day 4)

Embrace the Process to Define A "Higher" You

Fasting may or may not be new to you. Often, individuals become uncomfortable during a fast because it's something different. Change is considered a dirty word by some. The logic of "if it's not broken, don't fix it" has a positive and negative. Not being willing to change means you're not willing to follow God's will for your life, preventing you from manifesting the life you were born to live. Settling with expectations of it being temporary means you are content in your state, which is also an emotion of gratitude.

"Not that I speak in respect of want: for I have learned, in whatsoever state I am, therewith to be content."
- Philippians 4:11

For the next three days, embrace your experience with gratitude and be careful not to complain, which is an insult to our Heavenly Father. Embrace and expect the gift of learning "Simplicity" to appreciate the essentials and find joy in the basics of life.

Embrace and expect the gift of a "Body Reset" to become rejuvenated and sense a newfound vitality.

Embrace and expect the gift of "Mental Clarity" with more precise and better focus.

Embrace and expect "Emotional Balance" as a new resilience in facing challenges and maintaining a calm, centered state.

Embrace and expect "Appetite Insights." Understanding your body's valid hunger signals is a valuable lesson that transcends the fast. Embarking on this fast is a personal challenge that requires a deeper understanding of your purpose, path, and destiny. Embrace this journey to claim the life you were born to live!

YOUR CHALLENGE

Define the word **FAITH**:

____

____

____

Write two sentences using the daily word to claim the life you were born to live.

1)______________________________________

____

____

2)______________________________________

____

____

Define **YOU** in one positive word:

I AM___________________________________

"Ask, and it shall be given you; seek, and ye shall find; knock, and it shall be opened unto you!" - **Matthew 7:7**

Today's Affirmation

God knows my works and has set before me
a door no one can shut.
(Revelation 3:8)

Day 35

God's Word for You

If any of you lack wisdom, let him ask of God, that giveth to all men liberally, and upbraideth not; and it shall be given him. **-James 1:5**

Prayer

Our Father and our great God: The one who turns day into night and darkness into light. The God who created the sun, moon, and stars.

The God who can do anything but fail. All of my hope and all of my trust is in You. Guide and teach me the way that I should go. Order my steps in Your Word. Forgive me for my sins, and give me strength to endure. Sometimes, I feel unworthy, but Your Word says nothing can separate us from Your love. Thank You God! Help me honor You in all I do and say that others might see my good works and glorify You. Build a hedge of protection around us and give Your angels charge over us. May Your peace guide my heart and mind in Christ Jesus. In His precious name, I pray. Amen.

Fasting & Prayer (Day 5)

Can You See The Light?

There's an old saying, *"I can see the light at the end of the tunnel."* This is often said when something or someone gives you hope for the future after a long time of difficulty. Light symbolizes hope, guidance, joy, and life. It's the opposite of darkness, for **Psalm 30:5** says, *"Weeping may endure for the night, but joy comes in the morning."* Light is a sign that something beautiful is about to happen.

Our God has a history of turning darkness into light. **Mark 7:37** says He does all things well. He makes both the deaf to hear and the mute to speak. God is powerful, and His light shines brighter than the forces of evil. God took death itself and used it to redeem all of humanity.

He reached into the depths of our brokenness and began the restoration process. Stop trying to figure God's plan out and know He is mightier than any evil in this world.

Evil will never win. God can transform and revive every situation for our benefit and His glory. While not everything may appear good initially, God can weave all circumstances together for our ultimate good."

To love God, you must know Him, which begins with His Word. Think about this: How do you know what a person will and won't do if you don't know them? You can't have faith in someone you don't know. **Matthew 22:37** says:

"You must love the Lord your God with all your heart, soul, and mind. This is the first and greatest commandment."

Knowing God is the most significant decision you can make in your life. To love God, you must know him and live according to His purpose.

As you end the day, meditate on your experience during your five days of fasting & prayer. Reflect on things such as: was anything revealed or confirmed to you during this time, has your mind been renewed, and was your life impacted emotionally each day? I encourage you to continue prayer without ceasing and fast routinely to claim and manifest the life you were born to live!

YOUR CHALLENGE

Define the Biblical meaning of the word **REDEEMED**:

____

____

____

Write two sentences using the daily word to claim the life you were born to live.

1)____

____

____

2)____

____

____

Define **YOU** in one positive word:

I AM____

Today's Affirmation

I increase daily in wisdom, stature,
and favor with all men.
(Luke 2:52)

Day 36

God's Word for You

And they shall fight against thee; but they shall not prevail against thee; for I am with thee, saith the LORD, to deliver thee. ***–Jeremiah 1:19***

Prayer

Most gracious Heavenly Father: You alone are God, and there is no other God besides You. Thank You for allowing us to see another day. Thank You for Your grace and mercy. Thank You for loving us unconditionally. Thank You for keeping us from dangers seen and unseen. Thank You for fighting our battles. Forgive us, Father, for sins of commission and omission. Bless those who are sick, those in need, and those who are confused and discouraged. We come against anything that's not like You and ask that You would break every chain. Help us to know God that even when we don't know what tomorrow holds, we know who holds tomorrow. And greater is He that is within us than he that is in the world. Walk with us, Lord, and help us to know Your presence. In Jesus' name, we pray. Amen.

Count Your Blessings

Congratulations on completing your fast! It's time to reflect on your fasting experience. Consider writing in a journal about what you've learned, any insights you've gained, and how you felt during the fast. This will help capture your thoughts and feelings while they are still fresh in your mind. If you abstain from distractions such as TV and social media, continue to be intentional about their use. Consider setting aside a specific time for watching TV instead of having it on all day. In addition, try replacing background noise with uplifting music that resonates with your mission; however, be intentional in discerning hidden "negative" messages that could hinder your growth. This approach will keep your mind engaged positively.

Remember that your fast was about denying yourself and growing closer to God and His promises for you to claim. As you move forward, live with great expectation and patience. Remember, the end of a fast is not the end of the journey - it's a new beginning. May you continue to grow, seek God, and claim the life you were born to live!

YOUR CHALLENGE

Define the word **CHALLENGE**:

____

____

____

Write two sentences using the daily word to claim the life you were born to live.

1)____

____

____

2)____

____

____

Define **YOU** in one positive word:

I AM____

JOURNAL REFLECTIONS

FROM YOUR FASTING EXPERIENCE

Today's Affirmation

All that I am and all I ever hope to be,
I owe it all to God.
(Psalm 89:18)

Day 37

God's Word for You

And I say unto you, Ask, and it shall be given you; seek, and ye shall find; knock, and it shall be opened unto you. For every one that asketh receiveth; and he that seeketh findeth; and to him that knocketh it shall be opened.

- Luke 11:9-10

Prayer

Our Father and our Sovereign God, I give You thanks in all things. For every prayer You answered, every door You opened, every way You made, every time You healed, supported, rescued, forgave, delivered, and restored me. For these and all other blessings, I give You praise. In Jesus' name. Amen.

Guide to the Manifestation

Step 1: Ask with Faith & Humility

When asking to be blessed, you are communicating with a higher power. A supernatural favor that only God can give. A blessing is one of God's greatest gifts. It's a package waiting for you to claim. The requirement to claim your desires and blessings and to manifest the life you were born to live is to ASK.

You have not because you "ask not." When you don't ask, you forfeit blessings that have your name on them. God's bounty of abundance is limitless, and your life can be filled with miracles if you only ask. Asking can happen in several forms, such as prayer and meditation. The story of Jabez displays how God will place ordinary people on His honor roll. All it requires is you to ask. This action will grant you the ability to receive the blessings you desire. The number of blessings you receive is unlimited. Having more than one request doesn't mean you are greedy; it is a sign of faith.

God is ready and willing to take you to the next level by enlarging your territory. As your prayer requests are granted, you will undoubtedly know that it is only God. He has opened heaven's storehouse just for you. This will create joy inside that should be expressed through your praise and testimony.

Ask with humility by faith, and use godly wisdom to make the right choices.

YOUR CHALLENGE

1. Write what you want to ask God for. Be as detailed as possible.

"And the LORD answered me, and said, Write the vision, and make it plain upon tables, that he may run that readeth it." - **Habakkuk 2:2**

2. Add the Prayer of Jabez to your prayer journey daily.

"Oh, that thou wouldest bless me indeed, and enlarge my coast, and that thine hand might be with me, and that thou wouldest keep me from evil, that it may not grieve me!" –**1 Chronicles 4:10**

3. Display this Prayer somewhere you visit often to verbally and mentally transform your subconscious by faith.

Prayer Request

"And this is the confidence that we have in him, that, if we ask anything according to his will, he heareth us: and if we know that he hear us, whatsoever we ask, we know that we have the petitions that we desired of him."

-1 John 5:14-15

"Seek the LORD and his strength, seek his face continually." **-1 Chronicles 16:11**

"Watch and pray that ye enter not into temptation: the spirit indeed is willing, but the flesh is weak."

-Matthew 26:41

"And be not conformed to this world: but be ye transformed by the renewing of your mind, that ye may prove what is that good, and acceptable, and perfect, will of God." **-Romans 12:2**

"The LORD is nigh unto all them that call upon him, to all that call upon him in truth." **-Psalm 145:18**

"Continue in prayer, and watch in the same with thanksgiving." **Colossians 4:2**

Today's Affirmation

I am never alone.
(Isaiah 41:10)

Day 38

God's Word for You

Therefore, I say unto you, what things soever ye desire, when ye pray, believe that ye receive them, and ye shall have them. **-Mark 11:24**

Prayer

God of all mercies and compassion, creator and sustainer of all life: Thank You for Your amazing grace, work, and power. Thank You for Your faithfulness, love, and care. Thank You for Your great and tender mercies that are new every morning. Thank You for hearing and answering our prayers. Forgive us when we don't thank You enough. Help us see Your hand in our life with gratitude and reverence. Increase our faith and grant us eternal hope through Jesus Christ our Lord. In Jesus' name, I pray. Amen.

Guide to the Manifestation

Step 2: Expect with Faith & Action

You've made your request known by asking and improving the way you think. Now, it's time to take action. The biggest misconception of manifestation is assuming that positive thinking is enough. This is not an "instant" credit card process. Like Layaway, you must consistently go to a source to earn until the debt is paid to claim your reward. Taking even the most minor action toward your dreams will increase your odds of manifesting them. You must expect to receive what you asked and remember, *"Faith without works is dead."* - **James 2:26 (KJV)**

Ditch what's holding you back! Prepare for bumps on the road to success. Challenges will arise as you climb the ladder of success. Be confident in who you are in Christ and choose victory over defeat.

There is significant power in the repetition of words. Declare your desires out loud several times a day and write them down. This will help focus your mind on claiming and manifesting versus your current situation. Reinforce your request with the steps below as a guide to enlarging your territory.

- Create a vision board. Include images and quotes depicting your desires and goals for your life.

- If your goals are a part of a team effort, teach them what you have learned and request that everyone make it a part of their daily journey.
- Share the story about the Prayer of Jabez and your journey to Define You in God.

God will answer your prayers like He did for Jabez and many others.

YOUR CHALLENGE

Define the word **EXPECTATION**:

____

____

____

Write two sentences using the daily word to claim the life you were born to live.

1)______________________________________

____

____

2)______________________________________

____

____

Define **YOU** in one positive word:

I AM____________________________________

What actions have you started as you EXPECT whatever you ASK in Jesus' Name?

Today's Affirmation

I am walking in peace and abundance
by the grace of God.
(2 Peter 1:2)

Day 39

God's Word for You

Be careful for nothing; but in everything by prayer and supplication with thanksgiving, let your requests be made known unto God. And the peace of God, which passeth all understanding, shall keep your hearts and minds through Christ Jesus. **-Philippians 4:6-7**

Prayer

Most gracious God, our Heavenly Father: Thank You for allowing me to see another day. I know, God, that it wasn't because of anything great I've done but because of Your grace and mercy that I'm still here. Search me and know my heart; try me and know my thoughts. If anything in me is not like You, God, please take it out and cleanse me. Fill me with Your perfect love that casts out fear. Anoint me to forgive and honor You in all things. Wash me in the blood of Jesus. Fill me with Your Holy Spirit, and cleanse me from all unrighteousness. Thank You, God, for looking beyond my faults and seeing my needs. In Jesus' name, I pray. Amen.

Guide to the Manifestation

Step 3: Claim with Gratitude

Visualize your desires, act as if it's done, and give thanks.

"In everything, give thanks, for this is the will of God in Christ Jesus concerning you." **- 1 Thessalonians 5:18**

When you're obedient to God and express gratitude for what you have, you make space for more blessings. To attract abundance, you should also focus on blessing others. Holding onto things and hoarding can indicate that you don't expect new opportunities to come your way. By aligning your actions with your goals, you can prepare yourself mentally for the new blessings that are on their way. In the Sermon on the Mount **(Matthew 7:15–20 KJV)**, Jesus warns His followers of false prophets:

"Beware of false prophets, who come to you in sheep's clothing but inwardly are ravenous wolves. You will know them by their fruits."

It is essential to exercise patience and caution regarding our desires. Not everything that appears to be an answer to our prayers is meant for us. It could be a deceptive trap! Before claiming anything, we should ask ourselves, "What Would Jesus Do?" and consider our motives, honesty, laws, and other people involved. If any of these factors are questionable, it may not be a blessing from God but rather a trap from Satan. Anything that God provides will not come with negative consequences or strings attached. It should further God's ministry and help others come to repentance and faith in Him. The key is to focus on God and determine if the package aligns with His commandments.

The New Testament presents ten commandments that God has given to guide His believers towards a fulfilling life. These commandments are not intended to make life difficult; they are purposeful to help us be productive, reach our full potential, and enjoy a meaningful life.

Summary of the Ten Commandments

(Exodus 20:2-17 and Deuteronomy 5:6-21)

1. You shall have no other Gods before Me.
2. You shall make no idols.
3. You shall not take the name of the Lord your God in vain.
4. Keep the Sabbath day holy.
5. Honor your father and your mother.
6. You shall not murder.
7. You shall not commit adultery.
8. You shall not steal.
9. You shall not bear false witness against your neighbor.
10. You shall not covet.

I strongly encourage you to study each Commandment to define yourself further and identify what's yours to claim versus a counterfeit.

YOUR CHALLENGE

Define the word **CLAIM**:

____

____

____

____

____

Write two sentences using the daily word to claim the life you were born to live.

1)____

____

____

2)____

____

____

Do your goals align with the Ten Commandments?

Yes or No

Have you identified anything you've been doing incorrectly to claim and manifest your goals?

____

____

____

____

____

____

____

____

____

____

____

____

____

____

Define **YOU** in one positive word:

I AM______________________________

"And Jesus answering saith unto them, Have faith in God. For verily I say unto you, That whosoever shall say unto this mountain, Be thou removed, and be thou cast into the sea; and shall not doubt in his heart, but shall believe that those things which he saith shall come to pass; he shall have whatsoever he saith. Therefore I say unto you, What things soever ye desire when ye pray, believe that ye receive them, and ye shall have them."

- Mark 11:22-24

Today's Affirmation

I am victorious!
(1 Corinthians 15:57)

Day 40

God's Word for You

"And whatever you ask in prayer, you will receive if you have faith." - **Luke 1:37**

"For nothing will be impossible with God."
- 2 Corinthians 5:7

"For we walk by faith, not by sight."
- Romans 10:17

"So, faith comes from hearing, and hearing through the word of Christ."
- Matthew 21:22

Prayer

Father God, I know You didn't bring me this far to leave me. Thank You, in Jesus' name, that He whom the Son sets free is free indeed. Thank You for Your grace to overcome every hard trial. Thank You for the wisdom to look to Jesus. Thank You for forgiving me and transforming my life for Your glory. Today, I pray for the peace and strength only You can give. Help me to lean not to my own understanding but in everything to acknowledge You so that You can direct my words, thoughts, and actions. Help me recognize the lies of the enemy and rely on the truth of Your Word. Thank You that when I am weak, You are strong. Help me, Lord, to be full of faith, love, joy, peace, patience, gentleness, and self-control. Remind me that even when I can't see or hear You, you're always there, working everything together for my good. In Jesus' name. Amen.

The Fruit of Patience

Greatness doesn't happen overnight. Your efforts and courage to be brave and vulnerable, to face the unknown, are what matters. You must understand that in every failed attempt, there are lessons to help you claim and manifest the extraordinary life you were born to live.

Remember: Everything Happens for A Reason. Trust God and give Him time. Anything worth having is worth waiting for.

I believe God answers prayers in one of three ways:

1. Sometimes, God says, "Yes."
2. Sometimes, God says, "No."
3. Sometimes, God says, "Not yet."

Sometimes, when we pray, God answers our prayers in unpredictable ways greater than anything we could have imagined. Again, He knows what's best for us. Have you ever gone after something even though you knew it wasn't God's will for your life and regretted it? He can see much further than we can. Sometimes, His greatest gifts are unanswered prayers. As we navigate life, we may not understand how everything fits together. Still, we can trust that God has organized everything perfectly. Quitting is easy, and any goal you want to accomplish requires persistent actions. It's easy to see the problem and become defeated, but you must take your focus off the problem and focus on how you are going to reach your goal. Your mind is powerful, and saying "I can't" is what you will accomplish if that's what you believe. Do an honest inventory of yourself and pray to know what's preventing you from reaching your goals.

Once that is determined, you must revamp with a better strategy and try again. Being persistent is more than just doing something repeatedly. It means opening your mindset to the perception of your goals. You must talk only positive things and have several plans organized if plan "A" doesn't work. Your circumstances don't determine your future. Don't listen to negative people. Learn to recognize the voice of God. His Word is His will. Surround yourself with positive people who know how to get a prayer through. You can achieve it if you can perceive it.

You can't afford to leave your mind on auto-pilot because the mind has a mind of its own. Auto-pilot will get you in trouble if you habitually think negatively. Listen to your thoughts. Think about what you're thinking about and work towards changing your mindset. We can create our best life through the Power of Faith, Prayer, and Positive Thinking, with generous emotions of love, gratitude, and humility. All things are possible to those who believe.

"May the grace of the Lord Jesus Christ, the love of God, and the fellowship of the Holy Spirit be with you all."

- 2 Corinthians 13:14

YOUR FINAL CHALLENGE

Repeat the Process in Step 1. The manifestation process never ends. Reaching goals and losing focus during the process will put you at risk of losing your rewards. May blessings accompany you on your journey to claim and manifest the life God created you to live!

Today's Affirmation

It is God's will that I succeed and prosper.
(Psalm 37:4)

Made in the USA
Columbia, SC
10 January 2025

51478195R00111